Published in the United States by Fence Books, Science Library 320, University at
Albany, 1400 Washington Avenue, Albany, NY 12222,
www.fenceportal.org

Fence Books is a project of Fence Magazine, Incorporated, which is funded in part by
support from the New York State Council on the Arts and the National Endowment for
the Arts, along with the generous sponsorship of the New York State Writers Institute
and the University at Albany. Many thanks to these friends and to all Friends of Fence.

Fence Books are distributed by Consortium Book Sales & Distribution (cbsd.com)

and printed in Canada by The Prolific Group. (prolific.ca)

Cover art by C. F.
Cover design by Billy Merrell
Layout by Fence Books

Library of Congress Cataloguing in Publication Data
Legault, Paul [1985–]
The Other Poems/ Paul Legault

Library of Congress Control Number: 2011938405

ISBN 13: 978-1-934200-50-6

FIRST EDITION
10 9 8 7 6 5 4 3 2

THE OTHER POEMS

THE OTHER POEMS PAUL LEGAULT

THE 2011 FENCE MODERN POETS SERIES

ALBANY + NEW YORK ·

ACKNOWLEDGMENTS

I am grateful to the editors of the following journals in which some of these poems appeared:

Birdsong: "Noodles Are Forever," "Old People Who Don't Exist," "We Are Made Up of Smaller Versions of Ourselves…"

Boston Review: "Under the Gun," "Pomp & Circumstance," "Everything's First Time," "Get Out," "Lots of Birds and Lots of Mammals"

Maggy: "The Celestial Tradition," "The Great Greats," "New England is Old"

Offending Adam: "Como Mantequilla para los Católicos," "Missing You," "Wet Paint"

Supermachine: "Angela Lansbury Returns to Broadway," "Babes," "The Jungle," "Ranger Vs. Danger," "The Things You Find Underwater," "We Needed Monks"

Tuesday: "God Remembers the 90s"

Telephone: "[not good] [not hairy] [not not in bed] [not long]," "[load] [lyric] [lark] [lie] [louse]," "[underground] [under where you were standing] [under the control of your mind] [under the roof] [under your thumb]," "[not from] [not a] [not the place where they leave them alone]," "[a wave in the well] [closing one eye on cue] [closing one eye to convey a hidden meaning] [winkle-nook]," translated from the work of Uljana Wolf

Washington Square: "Free Twenty Dollar Bill," "Saturday Night"

+

"[not from] [not a] [not the place where they leave them alone]" was also included in Uljana Wolf's *False Friends* (Ugly Duckling Presse, 2011)

"The Senses," was presented at the New York Botanical Gardens as part of a literary walking tour sponsored by the Poetry Society of America and the National Book Foundation. It can be listened to by visiting the gardens, or calling: (718) 362-9561 x661

CONTENT

There You Go — 1
We Needed Monks — 2
Mishkin — 3
Company — 4
We Are Made Up of Smaller Versions of Ourselves Stacked Up On Top of the Smaller Versions of Ourselves' Shoulders Like a Human Ladder Wearing a Trenchcoat So That We Look Like Just "One Normal-Sized Person Coming Through Here, No Reason to Get Suspicious" — 5
Old People Who Don't Exist — 6
7. — 7
Lots of Birds and Lots of Mammals — 8
Hideaway Ranch — 9
The Circulatory System of a Bee in Spring — 10
The Sea Keeps Certain Things — 11
Empty Tub — 12
New England is Old — 13
Saturday Night — 14
110% — 15
The Oshawan Avant-Garde — 16
Shiny Things Inside of Other Shiny Things — 17
Free Twenty Dollar Bill — 18
Platform — 19
"Love is Like a Faucet" — 20
Worst Christmas — 21
OK — 22
Everything's First Time — 23
Ranger vs. Danger — 24
Babes — 25
Como Mantequilla para los Católicos — 26
Pomp & Circumstance — 27
Missing You — 28
Intermediate Algebra — 29
Wednesday Afternoon — 30

The Things You Find Underwater   31
Angela Lansbury Returns to Broadway   32
Women Who are Beautiful but Unhappy   33
For Little Paul   34
The Senses   35
Capulet   36
English   37
Baker's Dozen   38
The Principle of Relativity (in the Restricted Sense)   39
"Noodles Are Forever"   40
The Jungle   41
People Over the Age of Twenty Without Children   42
L'Amour Fou   43
Husband   44
Circular Breathing   45
Big & Close   46
Huge Lightning   47
Get Out   48
The Great Greats   49
Poem   50
Digital Weave   51
Incredible Winter   52
Guide to Tradition   53
When You're on the Go and You're Dad   54
The Proof of the Pudding   55
Dwarf Fortress   56
Pirate Ships on Fire = Gay   57
Animal Husbandry   58
The You-Know-What   59
Emotive Cello Music   60
Safety   61
Seventh Grade is for Losers   62
The Celestial Tradition   63
The Catch   64
Weather Is Good   65
Under the Gun   66
The Music from Inside   67
Sexual Pinocchio   68

God Remembers the Nineties   69
Wet Paint   70
[not good] [not hairy] [not not in bed] [not long]   71
[load] [lyric] [lark] [lie] [louse]   72
[underground] [under where you were standing]
    [under the control of your mind] [under the roof]
    [under your thumb]   73
[not from] [not a] [not the place where they leave them alone]   74
[a wave in the well] [closing one eye on cue]
    [closing one eye to convey a hidden meaning]
    [winkle-nook]   75

+

[title presenting a situation used to multiply the lines of thought] 77

the other is emerging as the necessary prerequisite for
dialogues with the self . . . I place myself there, with them,
whoever they are, wherever they are, who seek to reach
themselves and the other thru the poem by as many exits
and entrances as are possible.

—bpNichol

THERE YOU GO

At long last, I'm going in
with everybody.

EVERYBODY: Everybody, shut up.
MONDAY: It's happening again.
MONEY: It's me, isn't it?
A SYSTEM: Can I just say:

Run free in the wheat, commandant—
like a plow with a human face or

like a face plowing down the American plain.
SISTER-WIFE: I love you, other sister-wife.

BROTHER-HUSBAND: The stars are sitting down.
THE LITTLE CHAIR UNDERWATER: Be careful.

The widely celebrated reason for living
has just put on a hat.

WE NEEDED MONKS

But I don't know what for.
For groceries.

DAN: I need some monks.
STACY: I'm having a baby.
MONKS: Stacy's having a baby.
DAN: Stacy's having a baby.

Go from the yearly place, new Prime
Minister. There was a hem in it.

Lead with your hands to sight and to reckoning.
DAYTIME: Sometimes it is daytime.

STACY: Helen! Helen, I'm having—
HELEN: Stacy, oh my goodness—

Find a little bottle in a larger bottle
or you will be a poor man.

MISHKIN

Although you lead in from
underwater,

little Dan, I want something from you.
LITTLE STACY: So they say. Or at least something says so.
SOMETHING: I'm having something.
DAN: Something's having something.

Let it ride to it. Let the deck
get wet in Mississippi.

I had a time. Go to the place.
BOYCHICK: I will be good there.

LITTLE HELEN: Big Helen, why am I little?
THE PLACE: Oh, Little Helen. Little Helen.

Get along, ladybell. There was a fish once
or else there was just something there.

Inasmuch as she went to town,
she bought a hat.

NEW DANIELA: I want old Daniela.
OLD DANIELA: I resent you.
MAINE: I tried to be Mississippi
in the springtime in Maine.

If she came back to me, I think
I wouldn't be as lonely.

The spring in Maine is like a wet flame.
LUPE: That's what they all said.

THEY: No, we didn't.
MAINE: But you loved me.

Soon, there will be something
that was expected that put you there.

WE ARE MADE UP OF SMALLER VERSIONS OF OURSELVES
STACKED UP ON TOP OF THE SMALLER VERSIONS OF OUR-
SELVES' SHOULDERS LIKE A HUMAN LADDER WEARING A
TRENCHCOAT SO THAT WE LOOK LIKE JUST "ONE NORMAL-
SIZED PERSON COMING THROUGH HERE, NO REASON TO
GET SUSPICIOUS"

Whenever you were not going in from
the cold, you were gloveless.

SAPPHIRE: You had little hands
THE BUTCHER: And a sapphire.
THE CHILDREN: And a butcher.
THE MOTHERS: Give us our children.

In the spaceship, they were increasing
the parameter of experience

slowly. Back down, children.
THE LITTLE HANDS: Where are the little gloves?

THE LITTLE TRENCHCOATS: Are we alone?
THE MILES: We better stop.

I like that song that goes:
God only knows what I'd be without you.

Nevertheless she wouldn't
let down her hair.

HAIR: I am an extension of the dead.
EMPRESS: Light it up, light it down.
PAPA: Things don't always matter.
THE SUN: No, things don't.

Do something small and yellow, Nebraska. Nebraska,
inaugurate Arbor Day

by blowing, in summer, on my teenage ear.
CELIBACY: There is a pine tree.

PINE: I am your neighbor.
BOY: Boy, I'm going somewhere

where there's a distance
out of a distance that we had that we lost somewhere.

Concerning the inward movement going on here,
I don't like it one bit.

TYLER: There is something in my room.
AMBER: I am in your room, Tyler.
TYLER: There's something else there.
THE ROOM: Is it you, Tyler?

If something sounds red,
then rest assured
    it's in a language.

Repórtelo a un empleado de rojo o a un policia.
MICK: There has been an incident.

THE INCIDENT: I'm still happening.
MAN: I should be a bird in the mirror.

Doglight, doglight, what is up?
There is nothing but hardly ever.

If something's kind of sort of
something else, send it out.

DESSIRE: I will tell you if it's good.
LADY: I'm a magician or what I have turned into.
THE POOR: There is a second sort of life.
IMMIGRATION: As if you could remember

the first time you saw a car
    in a mirrored window.
Saints should drive blue cars

and stop at every light.
MICHAEL: I will wear my boots and khakis.

EAGLES: We are always looking for other eagles.
EAGLES: There you are—don't ever leave me again.

I'm tired of thinking
about the droves.

HIDEAWAY RANCH

The other thing being from another thing
entirely, X waits.

X: I'm not tired, I'm royalty.
THE GREEN FOOT: Let's get going.
THE CROWN: There are no foreigners.
THE FOREIGNER: There are no foreigners that exist.

There's trouble in trouble
and in Toledo.

Come here and love me.
WINTER: Shoosh.

THE HORSE IN WINTER: I am a figure.
THE BOUNDARIES: I had the dream about the cats again.

Tonight we will go from here to the border
at least.

In some way we will go there,
in, then under it.

SATURN: I want the Earth's moon.
THE MOON: It's my birthday.
THE CHRISTIANS: When will we die?
THE MOONS OF SATURN: Don't ask.

The way you lick your teeth
during the toothpaste commercial

is the only way, pilgrim-soldier.
THE ONLY WAY: I cannot see things.

KESTREL: If there are beautiful names...
RACHEL: Shut up and run.

Sometimes I need you to be my eyes.
Quick.

THE SEA KEEPS CERTAIN THINGS

Beyond the mall,
something else is starting.

PAM: I'm making my wish list.
PAM 2: Put me on it.
PAM 3: And a house made of watercress.
PAM: In which I will love you, Pam 3.

You should sleep on it in a field with the kings
as they consider their own ankles' strangenesses—

within my reach, within their little hives.
GOLD: Make everything me.

PAM 2: There is just enough room
     for me inside me.
GINGER: They go out, but then they come back.

Stairs always lead to more stairs.
Enough stairs make a house.

Where are you going, Jacques,
possibly constantly?

THE WHITE COTTON: There's something in my teeth.
THE U.S.S. FRANKLIN D. ROOSEVELT: <*foghorn*>
THE TEETH: I bit the other teeth.
YOU: If you can get along long enough in one place,

then you usually can't suddenly.
A bronze rope is a sculpture of a rope.

We could never have loved the earth—
GEORGE: If we had had no childhood in it.

DOG IN A HAT: We were made of pigeons.
PIGEONS: I was a dog in a hat.

Spring for us in spring exists as a placement
if not as a place.

After the first first late antiquity,
things are a little -ish.

THE BREAKERS: They are not soldiers.
THE SOLDIERS: You see I cannot see.
EMILY: They were a part of it.
THE SOLDIERS: They were not Emily.

Go through the hole to the nook,
little sister, send all your messages by mice.

Hurrying, there was a green light.
SYMBOL: I am a symbol.

THE LION AT THE LIBRARY: Listen up, Marilyn.
MARILYN: Bronze turns that dark color.

I took the train out. I just wanted
to see the boats in the snow.

SATURDAY NIGHT

Inside the place between it
and the window, you were looking alright.

SATURDAY: I feel it coming.
FERGUS: Who will ride with me?
WILLIAMS: What did you say was coming?
SATURDAY NIGHT: Saturday night.

I want my wife to be safe if there's a fever
or a balloon-ride.

If there's a bridge, they won't stop.
MY WIFE: Come off it.

THE LEGAL RIGHT: I am the legal right.
SATURDAY NIGHT: Saturday night!

There will be green things coming,
and there will be red things.

How dare you
invent God in a bathtub that you dreamt was a tower
    full of daisies made of flour in Spain.

SUMMER: Never trust a butler.
BADGER TOM: You're the only one who understands me.
POPE JOHN PAUL: This is it, badger.
BADGER JOHN PAUL: Can't you talk without pointing that gun?

In the confessional, there are ten buttons
a man you want to have sex with is pushing.

His name is Saskatchewan Saskatoon.
SASKATCHEWAN SASKATOON: You work here, angel?

ROSES: He would spend it on the ponies.
MAYAKOVSKY AS A PONY: And just why shouldn't he?

I am quite serious about the problematic nature
of suns wearing sunglasses.

At attention, they had the wherewithal
to manage the incoming—

GUNS: Rat-tat-tat-tat.
RAT-TAT-TAT-TAT: What?
BULLETS: Marry me to sound.
SOUND: I do.

Sometimes they would only come sometimes.
9:07:18 PM: The rabbits.

9:07:22 PM: The second rabbits.
9:07:36 PM: Blood on the telephone.

11:39:50 PM: Matthew's red socks.
11:40:00 PM: Something else.

There will be changes. They will say
how there were.

Notwithstanding a sort of loveliness
to the loveliness of horses, they hate you.

ROBERT FROST: Where should I put my hat?
THE INTERNET: I am behind you.
AUTUMN: Sometimes things die in me.
BEAR-CHILD: (*in a hat*) The way it hurts

when you look at things
underwater. FISH-CHILD: There is a king.

FISH KING: Who will be king of him?
BEAR KING: Kiss me in the mirror.

WATER: What time is it anyway?
WATER KING: Time to destroy the Earth,

or keep it for us, as if we had already
gotten around to having kept it.

FREE TWENTY DOLLAR BILL

From now on I'm going to be on parade,
and I will kiss all the beautiful men parading.

NIGHTTIME: I have this growth.
BETTY: This is my thinking time.
PANTHALASSA: Remember Panthalassa?
THE PARADE: The parade is a structure

if not in Paris then in a parade.
The Committee will bring you nuts wrapped in a napkin.

They will remind you of the hay on the floor at a dance.
SLOOP: I know there is a river.

MICHEL: C'est vraiment dégueulasse.
PATRICIA: Qu'est ce qu'il a dit?

I am going to watch a movie for a class.
Then I will eventually grow old and die.

In being sure of yourself, be sure
to eat like a thin pilot.

THE PRETTY BIRDS: We resent our beauty.
THE STRANGE ATTRACTORS: Nothing is invisible.
MAMA: Keep warm and other things too.
BASIN ST.: Mama, won't you tell me,

when I go, who will be there.
There is a violin playing over things

aggressively. There is usually a cat.
THE WEDDING: The sisters will give you.

GOD: I had a little trumpet.
THE LITTLE TRUMPET: There were these long weddings.

There were many brown cows, who could only be seen
in this one part of Spain, mainly at night.

"LOVE IS LIKE A FAUCET"

In my small potatoes,
there is a source.

HOUR: That was the same source that brought the whale.
MONTH: That was the source of the whale's daughter.
SPRING: That brought a desert.
THE WHALE'S DAUGHTER: That brought more desert.

Stop at the hilt. Some say
there is water inside of them.

The gambling hall shivers as the lady arrives.
HOME: If you stay, you can have me.

SHADE: There is a right answer.
TELEPHONE: I will live in a polished, golden ball.

I will drink from a polished, golden cup.
Sometimes a living creature will emerge.

WORST CHRISTMAS

Until the industrial revolution,
some animals were hitherto unknown.

DOG: I've never been to Atlantic City.
CAT: I've been to Catlantic City.
DOG: Oh, how is it?
CAT: You're not invited.

I've heard people die. I've heard
the moon has a French lisp

and a thick dart and a pillow and some pockets.
AUTUMN: How many pockets?

CAT: There are at least two.
THE MOON: Count again.

What were we drinking when they told us:
you don't need a gun in August?

OK

As long as they are tender in
the whale, it'll be okay.

HENRY: All these pipes above us.
HENRY: Like a river above us.
LIZA: The buckets will fill up.
LIZA: I will break all of the buckets.

I wanted a sister when I was younger,
now she's sixty-four in Arkansas.

They sent someone from the street to name us.
LACY: Call it Elaine.

ELAINE: There was a giraffe shot in the neck and the head.
1982: Don't touch me.

Sometimes you can see a system
of triangles in the landscape.

Of course you can have
whichever you prefer.

CALIFORNIA: The deer are both hatless and nude.
LA ROSA: I want an Irish birthday.
BASKET OF PUPPIES: What's in your basket?
BASKET OF FISH: I am not sentient.

At the cultural bureau, they've detected
that the bulls are all insolent and beautiful.

Sebastian usually rides through in the morning.
HIM: I will ride you to San Sebastian.

THE SUN: I will be a red nickel.
LOCAL FLORA: The flower-eating horses will eat us.

I would just like to say
the same thing again sometimes forever.

RANGER VS. DANGER

Up the creek, we met the sad men
with their paddles.

SAFETY: I will go last.
JOHN: John, be a good man.
JOHN: Kiss the other John, John.
JOHN: <kissing noises> ...

After you settle your accounts with the Wiccan monastery,
count me in.

The mines are filled with ballroom dancing.
THE ROOM WITH THE STONES: 1, 2, 3.

THE STONES IN THE ROOM: (ominous silence) ...
THE WATER IN IT: Steam can stop
    only momentarily.

At one point the bridge's arsonist was just
the person you saw on the bridge.

BABES

When you walk down the stairs at night in the city
your descent is set to trombone.

BLUE OX: I cannot show you my arms.
GOSPEL: Gimme some of that good gospel.
APPLES: There is a warm draft.
GAY CENTAUR: We should get coffee sometime.

The wick that runs through Joe Dallesandro is.
The new pots the drunken potter made are.

The gun in the motor is in the gun.
TAKE: 1. A teaspoon.

2. A bucket.
FILL: 1 then 2 repeatedly.

Children pretend to be tea cups.
Some men raise bees.

COMO MANTEQUILLA PARA LOS CATÓLICOS

Enough.
And enough again.

ATTENTION: Be on the look-out for a glass cabinet with a tallish man inside of it.
REWARD: White will not exist.
THE IMMORAL CITY: I am only Paris sometimes.
PARIS: Voudrais aller à la plage.

The sound of memory is sevenths multiplying
like juice projected onto a gong

on a hot day the sun went down on.
ORAL SEX: I will be your invisible sister.

SEX: Sister, it's your wedding day.
MOM: This poem is inappropriate.

I'm sorry, mom.
I don't really know.

In the midst of all this hubbub over God's bisexuality,
the wedding DJ tried to kill himself.

HETERONORMATIVE MALE #1: I'd have sex with God.
SARTRE: I'd let him fuck my tits.
HETERONORMATIVE MALE #2: I'm more of a Joan Crawford kind of guy.
JOAN CRAWFORD: Every film should have a bathtub scene.

Simplicity isn't necessarily the answer
to the great and hypothetical question of

how to stage a naked-lady-gun-show.
BUSBY BERKELEY: I want the dancers to be limp.

BUSBY BERKELEY: Invisible men will carry them.
BUSBY BERKELEY: When they are shot from the cannons

we must see where they land,
then where they live, and the rest of their lives.

MISSING YOU

From the rafters, they lowered an angel with the head of a dog and no legs
    or arms, that flapped around with its wings for a bit until it got tired, at which
    point it just laid there, barking angrily and then whimpering until it fell asleep
    sometime in the night and dreamt of mustangs
and of rivers and of death.

CHRISTINE: Oh. Hi there.
WAYNE: He reminds me of West Virginia.
WEST VIRGINIA: He reminds me of you, Wayne.
THE WINGS: I wish wings had thumbs.

Surprisingly enough, someone invented badminton
and cheese, and England, and science fiction.

They should have a parade.
ELIZABETH TAYLOR: Men should wear pearls more often.

COYOTES: I'm afraid of the snow.
THE SNOW: I get very nervous.

It could just be all the shit we were doing.
Or it could be anywhere.

Inside the door and to the left,
everything's incoming.

THE PINK WHEAT: They've tied the ribbon to the house.
CORAL: My wife and her are white.
CATARACT: Send out the messenger in March.
BASTILLE: You raise up
    the king poles.

Have him.
Have had dinner.

Then begin by having been running already.
RESERVATION #1: I don't like people.

PEOPLE: People say I'm crazy.
PANTS: The duality of progress will deter us,
    but from what exactly?

We read a book.
A kissed me and B.

As you know, it goes all the way
like a nail through the button.

MULTITUDES: I want to be restless and big.
FACT: A donkey could ride on an elephant
    if he had had proper training.
AIR FORCE: Rigor is the key to unlocking a succession
    of pleasures in the agent of rigor.
THE AGENT OF RIGOR: Like gold poured over a notch.

Fernando, Fernando, Fernando, Fernando,
poppies want you when they don't want me.

Nature never built a container.
FIRE: What would you have us do?

PILGRIMS: You can burn milk.
CROQUETTE ON THE BEACH: The only person who could ever love Friday

was Elizabeth Bishop.
Crusoe must have made his little shoes.

THE THINGS YOU FIND UNDERWATER

Now that we're on the level,
I'm unsure of where we were before.

JACQUES COUSTEAU ON THE BEACH: Put me back.
HISTORY: Give me that stick.
BIOLOGY: Give me that small shoot or branch, separated as by a cutting.
HELEN OF TROY: Things can be boring-boring or interesting-boring

like a spotted partridge eating toast
versus the stupid faces I made

when I was alone with the cats.
AMAZONIA: Who needs curtains?

FLORAL PRINT DRESS: I will kill all my slaves.
MANATEE: Do it but do it

when we were young.
An octopus's butt is also its mouth.

Ever since January, I am always
seriously about to kill something.

MATADOR: Come along, mi faro cubano.
APPRENTICE: The exactness of your pants will bury Greek drama
    in its hall of coats lit by matchlight.
LARAINE: I really enjoy helping children develop into healthy young adults.
JESSICA: Suck my dick, Laraine.

The rice in the Petri dish
is about to pop.

We could do anything. Anything could do us.
TRAVIS: I'm having a secure feeling.

DEATH: That's exactly what we are going to do.
CHIMERA: I understand now.

Put that dog back in the cupboard.
Give that beautiful woman unheard-of power.

WOMEN WHO ARE BEAUTIFUL BUT UNHAPPY

At five till one they will stop talking
so their eyes can rake the silt.

EMILY: Happiness would be my downfall.
VICTORIA: It hurts to boogie.
ISADORA: Looking up takes time.
WET CLAY: Tie me to a chair.

The pipes are standing at the back of the theater.
No one knows what to do tonight.

They are plotting to keep me
    in the new year.
O: The trees can gallop.

ALICE: But what's the endpoint?
HEDDA: My socks are too short.

My dress is alive.
Get it off.

FOR LITTLE PAUL

When you are probably and old,
second-guess it.

THE SITE: I am not specific.
PAUL: I would like to be.
K$_0$: You don't have to be dead to see me.
GRANNY: You do not have to be

anything at all.
If you were older, you would be giving me

advice about things that you know about.
TEXAS WHEN IT RAINS: Like the way a train goes and has a shadow.

THE KINKS: Where did my bones go?
YOSHI: I will lick through the walls

to get to you.
Your Nanna's dog's name was Ginger.

THE SENSES

Then they made another garden
but differently.

FRAGRANCE: There's always something in color.
TEXTURE: There are always bird walks.
SOUND: There are turkeys on these grounds
     and José the Beaver
     far off in the forest without thoughts.
AUDIO TOUR GUIDE: There is almost always

an irregular ball
     about two feet high
described on this phone-line.

In the future, or in three months, the plants will change,
     or else they will be about to have to.
THE FUTURE: Who senses me when I'm not there?

LAVENDER: The bed is knee-high
     and lined with a single wall.
WANT: You want to grow your own food,

annihilating all that's made,
and live in Paradise alone.

CAPULET

No one loves you.
Nothing you touch
    will catch fire immediately.

MEL: Still, you can plan your garden
    to look like a face.
DAISIES: I will make a web where the ground breaks down.
CATTLE: Men have made hills in peacetime.
YOUR MOTHER IN YOU: Bring me the coordinates.

The fact of the matter
is quite striking.

It takes a minute
    before it takes an army.
SOME: We believe in a song in theory.

MOST: I can't dance.
LUCY: Take off your ivy

in a straw hat in the Catskills.
Maybe use your ruby knife.

ENGLISH

A little light
and now.

A RINGING BELL: Maybe at last they'll start up.
BEYOND: They are the machines.
CENTRAL HEATING: They are the machines under the palms.
ROBINSON: I had the same things—

cigarette papers, etc.
The datebook says

what you thought about.
FLOWER MARKET: Grow out your certainties.

GALLERIES: If you love it, it will flatten.
HEAD: The heart beats mostly.

How to change:
I want everything.

BAKER'S DOZEN

Instead of bread,
I'm going to make some sense.

MORE: Throw everything in for good measure.
ELVIS: Pick me up by the handle.
COURTESAN: Do it whether I'm Mayan or not.
ECHO: I will be the sea's oven.

There is the remarkable tragedy that
you can't live in Iceland

at the same time you live in Spain.
WET CAKE: Butter isn't a form of transportation.

CHARITY: Unless this is your stop.
YORBA LINDA: I feel daily and imminent.

Means stop.
Stops stop.

Now, in virtue of its motion,
is going to happen again.

EARTH WHEN SHE WAS YOUNG: It's like you could ride me.
BABY BIRD: Say lightning strikes
    the rail in two places.
BABY FOX: One is not possible alone.
BABY ANIMAL: I am a simultaneity

like Germany,
and a lot of things,

and the wheels they hid under the deck.
BUSTER: It's hard to dance when you're eating.

PAT: <*the sounds of the rain forest*>
JAMES: When I saw the Queen

I was running at her
with you in my arms.

By order of everything,
there are a lot of low expectations.

CELIBACY: People are like children.
THINGS: We can always go wrong.
SOUTHERN PEOPLE: What I ain't ain't much.
A WET STRING: That's what you sound like.

The landscape is holy if its birds take to water.
The foam curls at the sea beast's feet.

I don't even know who you are most of the time.
BEAR-CHANDRA: You were going to be me.

MOLLY: Take me away
    through the mud's black speculum.
ORGANS: One thing at a time.

Nothing's not normal. Never mind
how you were thinking about not thinking about it.

THE JUNGLE

These days, people hallucinate a little slower.
There's something wrong with me or without me.

RUSSIAN PINEAPPLES: Keep us warm, Vladimir.
TEA: I would like some more tea.
THE SUN: Put some whiskey in it.
THE PARTY BUS: If we continue

down this path to a convergence
of the external with its twin—

which can be done simply enough—
MAJESTY: Then I'll have finally made it.

REGALITY: From little to nothing.
CHANGE: For good

for once,
forest.

How do I sound
or how can Holly jump from her moving vehicle
    in the marshes if the marshes get thick there.

LATENESS: Things aren't bad.
ABSENCE: I'm pretty good.
PREEMPTIVITY: I'm that like a jackknife.
JACK OF DIAMONDS: I'm that like the clubs.

Vertically speaking,
I live here.

Horizontally, I'm more of a Southerner.
CHARLES: (*sleepily*) Faith is tall
    and slowly filling with milk.

TORTOISESHELL GLASSES: Like the way corn is.
SIGHT: Or like the tulips in the corn,

or how they're yellow like you'd be
if you were corn or the tulips in the corn.

L'AMOUR FOU

Seriously, we cannot attach any meaning
to you riding off
   on a dog
    to the old wars in the new middle territories.

LINCOLN: It's always about half an hour until something happens.
LINCOLN: But I don't know which half.
JOSHUA SPEED: American landscape painting is the new real thought.
OLD PEOPLE: A fish-ghost is turning into a human one.

Lewis never wanted Clark to marry him,
but he would've liked it

for them to have had children
OREGON: Strangeness seems good.

LOUISIANA: Hold the convict by his hair.
THE PLAINS: One thing leads to another in a race.

Prince Charming wouldn't have needed to exist
if Sleeping Beauty had cut off her hands.

HUSBAND

Either your animal isn't around anymore
or its not yours at all.

PAINTED CAT: Either way you knew which one it was.
HUMAN SOUL: I forget what I think about oranges.
CAT SOUL: I don't understand what candy is.
LEGACY: I don't have hands.

The wolfman chisels his silhouette against
    the stucco of the orange piazza.
Sven built things underwater

so that he could live there.
SVEN: I would like to unrelease me.

STOP: Most people should be nineteen.
NINETEEN: I am only just now noticing

how the trees smell like semen in April.
Some wings have additional wings.

CIRCULAR BREATHING

Same old jazz piccolo.
Same old biscuits.

SAME OLD: Third story .
SAME OLD: The new prison.
SAME OLD: Songs don't like you.
SAME OLD: Tale about the bird baking bread.

Same old Sam got older same as
same old Irma did.

Same old things get closer.
SAME OLD: Thing.

SAME OLD: Same old.
SAME OLD: When you're a person.

Same old being old
when you're an old person.

Whatever.
Whenever too.

INTEGRITY: Pay the mermaid in glances
    or in just the idea of debt.
JUSTICE: Lightning can't get cancer.
RECREATION: People collect bones.
TRUTH: I want to be the best wig

and to be taken off
and put on a person
    in sequins at midnight who will love me, drunk,

like a mother loves the idea of ancestry.
CALIBAN: I don't know why I'm still in New York.

ELEVEN YEARS: I'm a singer-songwriter.
PERFORMANCE: Water comes from the ground.

I've always been sensitive.
Put it back.

HUGE LIGHTNING

Until you do right by me,
your life will be like a white suit is
    when you're flying, in the rain, which you caused.

FAT STORM: Water remembers you.
HORSES: I can't talk right now.
CAPITOL: Start here and hurry.
PLAINNESS: You know that you have too much milk

when you start to require a compass
and a team, and something to be golden and lost.

Captains can't hunt for butterflies.
CAPTAINS: I'm not sure if my feelings are powers.

BABY: I need your loving.
BABY: I got to

have all
of it.

In Montreal and indoors
Montreal is overcome with lateness.

CARMINA: Step lively and then to the left.
TRENT: Stand still completely for once.
DOLLHOUSE: Sometimes you can only move your eyebrows.
PEOPLE DRESSED AS HOUSES: Windows are not always not doors.

There is a high-pitched noise in the taqueria
that makes it difficult intermittently

to think of how we've made a Quebec of ourselves.
BIRD ISLAND: That's not Québec.

ISLAND HOUSE: That is not the sea-place
    they saw there.
QUÉBEC: I have a few more in me.

One has been led off out of habit.
One wonders where one should've gone.

THE GREAT GREATS

Together or toward us
there is more use and a greater chance
    that there will be more things
    that are unowned.

DUSTY TAXIDERMIC RABBIT: Your footprints look like shoes.
BASEMENT: I can see your inner basement.
DINING ROOM: You hold yourself carelessly.
CANDELABRA: Auden never wore underwear,

was never young,
never learned to walk, came out already knowing

how to talk with a pipe in his mouth.
AUDEN: I developed my palette
    the way a fly sharpens a sword.

PERSPICACITY: Make sure you smell like gunpowder.
PROSPERO: Talk in your sleep about the billboards.

The billboard says:
"What does the billboard say?"

POEM

To do so
or to don't.

BELLY: Time takes time.
LADIES IN WAITING: King us.
WAITING ROOM: Can't do.
PEOPLE THAT LIVE IN CASTLES: The targets at night

that were undone at night
were not the only targets at night.

The dead priestesses are increasing.
UNDEAD PORPOISE: I want my keep.

OCEANIA: Call me.
BOILED FLOWERS: Call them

Grace Jones when she is beautiful
or Grace Jones on fire when she is.

For all futurity, we'll go following
the future of literature to itself.

BRANDON: If I'm from a pink sort of London
    the whole thing seizes up.
WHITE LEGUME: Run out.
CARNIVOROUS FOREST: Spread out
    like dice.
SEVEN: I'm coming.

You look better than you do.
Do they hold it in?

Are they a little summer coat?
BEST: Best me.

IT: Take it away.
THEY: Are they a little summer fort

in Tennessee? Are they how
you can't see buildings inside of them?

Given a condition that is assumed to be true without further evaluation,
things stay sound.

DANCER: There is a twenty-year-old being living with us.
SPECIALTY: They put me in my case.
CASE STUDY: Before you forget, you have to start to.
ATLAS: Here went here. Here

looks to be in order now. Here
looks like a hand pretending to be a duck

from the lakes.
PETER: When having a three-way, don't leave.

PAUL: Don't leave it up to yourself.
MARY: Things are getting

uphill both ways
inside.

In that the Confucian Great Learning
is an examination with a clear purpose—

THE EXAMINATION OF MOTIVATION: I am a root.
THE CENTRE: Of steadily out-circling causations.
IMMEDIATE ORDER: From me.
A WHOLE SERIES OF HARMONIES AND GOOD CONDUCTS: To me.

Ezra Pound pivots.
The seven. sages

reiterate our debt.
CIVILIZATION: Go.

THE IMPERIAL COURT: Go be a mixture of perfumes.
YOUNGHUSBAND: When I got to Lhasa

I found Connecticut there
in Connecticut's mouth.

Leftovers
again.

DAD: My wife is your mom.
WILF: I'm your dad's dad.
DAD: Your dad is me.
DAD: Once my mother threw a bowl of spaghetti.

Once my grandparents married
    each other's cousins.
I used to walk to the local mountain.

Cake was made back into cake.
DAD: Enjoy each day.

DAD: Sometimes I like to be alone.
DAD: Once I watched a friend die on Mt. Everest.

I was your age
    and you were my son.
I will be dead when you are.

THE PROOF OF THE PUDDING

Ever since, it's been so long
that it barely fits in its place.

WOMEN WITH UNCONVENTIONALLY LONG HAIR: We are not all a little off.
COOKIE: You can't learn less.
WET FOOD: You'll ruin your dress, cookie.
MACARTHUR PARK: I want you inside of me

like a box wants respectable contents.
Pretend the refrigerator's packaging

is the refrigerator.
VEGETABLES THAT LOOK LIKE BODY PARTS: Faces are pieces.

WEATHER: Doors swell.
WEATHER: Weather's hungry.

Like a box
made of weather.

After that, Mike keeps getting thirsty
and then almost dying of it.

KIVISHIDENLUSLEM: Let me describe myself.
KIVISHIDENLUSLEM: She's always tense and jittery.
KIVISHIDENLUSLEM: She's slow to anger.
KIVISHIDENLUSLEM: She's very active.

Her somewhat tall ears are somewhat narrow.
Her somewhat narrow head is somewhat tall.

She is a citizen of the remarkable diamond.
KIVISHIDENLUSLEM: She is a member of the infinite boulder.

KIVISHIDENLUSLEM: She has a good awareness of her emotions.
KIVISHIDENLUSLEM: She starts to stutter when she gets angry.

She has the appearance of somebody who is sixty-years-old
who isn't and is one of her kind.

PIRATE SHIPS ON FIRE = GAY

In this situation, my main squeeze
has gotten just about everywhere.

THE QUEEN PRINCE: Behead the violet flowers
    that aren't violets.
PRINCE: Prince's childhood nickname was "Skipper."
BLUEBEARD: Behead the red cannons. And it is spring.
BLUE: Red means don't.

Lead the white eel.
A partridge could come in.

She greatly appreciates art and natural beauty.
XANDER: But who is she?

LUCAS: You mean *Her*?
HER: I am the captain's rooms' invasion.

There is a hook pulling the horizon off.
Men walk other men's planks.

ANIMAL HUSBANDRY

On the beat and on wheels,
I do this thing called beach patrol.

DARNELLE: What are you wearing?
HORSE 1: Ice pink and chocolate plaid with ice lavender and Sahara accents.
HORSE 2: Ice green plaid with Sahara and chocolate accents.
HORSE 3: Ice blue plaid with ice green, hunter, and cream accents.

The anthropomorphic cat eating the non-anthropomorphic mouse
doesn't really want to. Or else he wanted to inside somewhere

where he couldn't admit it.
OLD BEAGLE: I remember sans memories.

RED OCTOBER: The ice paddle serves its purpose.
GALAPAGOS: Last season should've been the last season that

some wooden mass set sail
when I was on it.

THE YOU-KNOW-WHAT

Despite itself,
the criticism is happening in time.

8:53: I think that.
8:54: I don't.
SPRING: Come get my chicken.
DAZE: There is a difference

between waiting for the scenery to quit
looking at itself chewing on something

and not.
SEBASTIAN: What did you hide off into, Sebastian?

SEBASTIAN: An Elvis made entirely of pollen.
REDWOOD: And an Elvis made of tissue paper

arm in arm
with the luminary.

Under the weather or not,
the meteorologist's annoyed you called him that.

1ST CHAIR: I want to be 2nd chair.
WOODEN CHAIR: I want knees.
WOODEN TEMPLE: What I got's yours.
BUDDHA: I only invented the lama

so the monks could have a baby.
Will people go jogging

when there are only 200 of them left?
CORMAC: Whose following is crouched in the bushes?

DIANA: They are all wearing seriously red pants.
NANCY: My dad only wears his marathon T-shirts

in the whole world. Where's the fire
in the whole world?

Anyway,
and then she says—

KAREN: Get this.
MATH: Got it.
CHEMISTRY: I feel you.
MR. ASHBY: I feel mustered into the service of the United States
    during the late Civil War.

The plants and birds are pretending to be
    each other again.
The power to kill thinks it's a green duck

who doesn't believe in wind power.
TURBINE: Bring me the man from La Mancha.

WINDJAMMER: Love's flag is actually a sail.
CADET: I'm currently not losing you.

But then what?
And after that?

Between you and me,
get up.

SILENCE: What color am I?
GOLD:
GOLD:
GOLD: I want to be for cash

the way cash is for me.
The way exchange is necessary to willing

change into existence.
CHANGE: I mean a lot.

SIEGFRIED SASSOON: Who murdered the daffodils?
VIDAL SASSOON: Whose hair is that

on the bench?
I don't like it.

Alongside or rather a long way from
alongside of factual study, it runs.

ETC.: The homosexual undertones of Apollo 11.
THE CAERULEUM COELUM: Better be back soon.
THE AUGUSTUM COELUM: Betty, let me in.
THE 2000 YEARS: Leave me alone.

It's spring and everyone is eligible
especially the men on TV

who are getting mad again
        about the internet.
THE GREEK: Sculpture is always an erosion.

PLATO: Press on the world like a curtain.
GLORYHOLE: Come to the world

with your boots on forward,
then come to it backwards.

THE CATCH

being that you may perhaps not like it
at all.

THE CHILDREN: I don't like it.
IT: You don't have to.
HELL: Where's that moth that makes my heart a dancer?
THE CHILDREN: In the cupboards.

Bears, when eating their or someone else's
children, don't ask first.

Some things come on strong.
DANGER: I'll be gentle.

OLD MAN JENKINS: I love you.
OLD MAN LEGAULT: I love you too.

You should be my place that is an old man
who I am in love with.

WEATHER IS GOOD

Shut up when it's so good.
My computer has computer friends.

COMPUTADORA: I am also the animals.
THE OLD WELL: I feel socially anxious.
BENITO: I forget if they hung or shot us.
MAY: Now that it's summer enough

at the top of the stairs,
you found a sandal

with some blood on it.
ELEANOR: That's not mine.

DOROTHY: I don't have enough sanity.
SUMMER: Ok. Ok,

already, guys.
Jig's up.

When this sentence should speak for itself,
it does the way it does

everything: more or less.
FACTORY: We make the same moves on each other.
DALLAS: Get me the monkey.
ORANGUTAN: I prefer: 'person of the forest'
    or else 'reference point.'

The camping party entered
not only the entrances.

Somebody took the cake.
J. PUCKLE: Good thing it wasn't God.

GOD: I wouldn't have given it back.
THE LITTLE BASSOON: I want to experience the unfinished works
    of Paul Valéry,

the way life unfinishes like a ghost,
all over your face.

Emo or not,
I'm still a cop.

GARFIELD: There is a root in things.
ODIE: And a golden knot.
THE AUTHORITIES: (*with their sadness*) And the animals who are read about.
OPTION #1: Send a "Carve Your Heart Out Yourself"

ringtone to your cell
thanks to fatboy_418@yahoo.com,

pinkyrl41@yahoo.com, and callou2@aol.com.
OPTION #2: Lift the top off.

GREECE: Your haircut makes you look sensitive.
THE MALL: I'm going to take you,

the way a Tennesseean witch takes a pill,
straight.

Of the week,
and its best, they named you—

THE COMMITTEE: 'Sexual Pinocchio of the Week.'
BEACHED WHALE IN A DARK ALLEY: There you go.
CORRELATE: I am the correlate.
THE ACCOMPLISHED MUSICIAN: On the other side of the mountain,

I play like a genius.
If a donkey stops twice,

listen up.
THE FOREST: Get me the wooden doctor.

A REAL BOY: When the boys get rowdy,
    you better get going.
BFF: What are you doing here, JTT?

Oh.
No. No, thank you.

GOD REMEMBERS THE NINETIES

Everybody has been hanging around here
a lot.

ANITA: I stubbed my toe on the ottoman.
JEAN-BERTRAND: I touched myself in the eye.
A LAMP: If there is music, there is a room.
WIKIPEDIA: Some people are listening to "The Dolphin's Cry."

I cannot think of anything sadder
than your parents' clothes in a suitcase—

besides the mass production of spoons.
DOLLY (THE SHEEP): If the world had a face, I'd spit on it.

LOVE (THE SHEEP): I'm famous for being famous.
THE CARNIES: Philosophy can be a means

of exploring joy and its intricacies.
There is a wooden bird that drinks water.

WET PAINT

Before we knew it, everyone had
at least kissed a cousin.

THE BEACH: Simplicity is for strangers.
BIRTH: I like to watch the beach give me
    to shells and the living citizens.
CANDACE: I like to collect leaves.
CANDACE'S BONES: Shake, shake, shake.

Boston is asleep in its sepulcher.
Robert and Robert died

like two angry virgins hoisted off
    into the same white bonnet.
STEVIE: I put my sugar in the pail.

ROBOT CHEF: I will light the blue torch.
DOLLY PARTON: They will have to fill a canyon with rhinestones

to ever really get rid of me.
I laid my white egg in the flood's white center.

[NOT GOOD] [NOT HAIRY] [NOT NOT IN BED] [NOT LONG]

Soon and soon and in between
something's at it again.

HAIR: Don't touch me.
THEMSELVES: I can't.
THEM: Neither can we.
NEITHER: But I can.

Take a mountain,
for example,

or just take one.
GOLD: Put me in your mouth.

HEDGEHOG: Hold me as tight as I would hold you
    if only I had hands.
HARE: If I had hands, I'd stop running.

If your hair had hands it would want to touch you
on the cheek, on the other hand.

A-
hem.

MOUTH: There's a throat in my neck.
LOG: I'm not going to take anything
    lying down.
PINOCCHIO: I am a woodwind instrument.
BOY: <*buzzing noises*>

The song goes.
You are a burden.

Stay tuned for more information.
THROAT-SINGER: Why can be a reason.

A CLEARING: Listening spreads.
ONSLAUGHT: I'm going

to be happening.
Now I'm happening.

[UNDERGROUND] [UNDER WHERE YOU WERE STANDING] [UNDER THE CONTROL OF YOUR MIND] [UNDER THE ROOF] [UNDER YOUR THUMB]

After becoming a hobo,
I thought about the trains
    and your preciousnesses.

TRAIN 1: The noise of the train.
TRAIN 2: Das lärmen der züge.
GRASS TRAIN: What am I?
GRASS THRESHOLD: Green.

Despite being unmovable,
yonder on the storage track,

it's slippery.
PLATFORM: Lean out.

PRACTICE: Give me an example.
PLATFORM 2: That's easy.

The sun
in the morning.

[NOT FROM] [NOT A] [NOT THE PLACE WHERE THEY LEAVE
THEM ALONE]

At the zoo, them being the animals at the zoo,
it being the zoo, it was closed.

MISTER: What'll it be?
TEETH: To be a train
    that's been let out.
ZEBRAS: There was a kind of zoo once.
ZEBRAS: Now there is just this zoo.

Everything is its separate everything.
We discovered the lizards

are not exactly dancing.
GINGER: Let's call the whole thing—

FRED: No.
YOU: I like you

like them
but on the way home.

[A WAVE IN THE WELL] [CLOSING ONE EYE ON CUE]
[CLOSING ONE EYE TO CONVEY A HIDDEN MEANING]
[WINKLE-NOOK]

Were I the princess of snails,
they'd call me Lady Wentletrap.

FLOTSAM: Life happens inside.
THE SEA: Then it builds out.
THIEF: There were white stairs on the beach.
THE WHITE STAIRS: It's hard to land

after living here.
They send you from the dark corners

into science.
MERMAID: I'll turn my cheeks their alien green.

ANTENNAE: I'll look at you, knowingly.
GOOD: I don't know if I'm going to occur.

I want to end my life like
swoosh.

[TITLE PRESENTING A SITUATION USED TO MULTIPLY
THE LINES OF THOUGHT]

[Prepositional statement opening into the continuation
of the second line to the end of the first sentence]

SUBJECT: (*descriptor*) [Statement of personal action]
OBJECT: [Apology]
COUNTER-OBJECT: [Counter-statement]
NEW THOUGHT: [Order

put forth to
the absent audience

addressed to perform a new action]
IMPLIED SUBJECT: [Agreement]

MEDIATOR: [Question without interrogative punctuation]
FUTURE SUBJECT: [Directions

on how to place the verbal processes
in relationship to the reader's final adjustment of the text]

Fence Books has a mission to redefine the terms of accessibility by publishing challenging writing distinguished by idiosyncrasy and intelligence rather than by allegiance with camps, schools, or cliques. It is part of our mission to support writers who might otherwise have difficulty being recognized because their work doesn't answer to either the mainstream or to recognizable modes of experimentation.

The Motherwell Prize is an annual series that offers publication of a first or second book of poems by a woman, as well as a five thousand dollar cash prize.

The Fence Modern Poets Series is open to manuscripts by poets of any gender and at any stage of career, and offers a one thousand dollar cash prize in addition to publication.

Fence Books is also a participating publisher in the National Poetry Series.

For more information about these prizes, or about *Fence*, visit www.fenceportal.org.

THE MOTHERWELL PRIZE

Negro League Baseball	Harmony Holiday
living must bury	Josie Sigler
Aim Straight at the Fountain and Press Vaporize	Elizabeth Marie Young
Unspoiled Air	Kaisa Ullsvik Miller

THE ALBERTA PRIZE

The Cow	Ariana Reines
Practice, Restraint	Laura Sims
A Magic Book	Sasha Steensen
Sky Girl	Rosemary Griggs
The Real Moon of Poetry and Other Poems	Tina Brown Celona
Zirconia	Chelsey Minnis

FENCE MODERN POETS SERIES

The Other Poems	Paul Legault
Nick Demske	Nick Demske
Duties of an English Foreign Secretary	Macgregor Card
Star in the Eye	James Shea
Structure of the Embryonic Rat Brain	Christopher Janke
The Stupefying Flashbulbs	Daniel Brenner
Povel	Geraldine Kim
The Opening Question	Prageeta Sharma
Apprehend	Elizabeth Robinson
The Red Bird	Joyelle McSweeney

NATIONAL POETRY SERIES

A Map Predetermined and Chance	Laura Wetherington
	selected by C. S. Giscombe
The Network	Jena Osman
	selected by Prageeta Sharma
The Black Automaton	Douglas Kearney
	selected by Catherine Wagner
Collapsible Poetics Theater	Rodrigo Toscano
	selected by Marjorie Welish

ANTHOLOGIES & CRITICAL WORKS

Not for Mothers Only: Contemporary Poets on Child-Getting & Child-Rearing
Catherine Wagner & Rebecca Wolff, editors

A Best of Fence: *The First Nine Years, Volumes 1 & 2*
Rebecca Wolff and *Fence* Editors, editors

POETRY

June	Daniel Brenner
English Fragments A Brief History of the Soul	Martin Corless-Smith
The Sore Throat & Other Poems	Aaron Kunin
Dead Ahead	Ben Doller
My New Job	Catherine Wagner
Stranger	Laura Sims
The Method	Sasha Steensen
The Orphan & Its Relations	Elizabeth Robinson
Site Acquisition	Brian Young
Rogue Hemlocks	Carl Martin
19 Names for Our Band	Jibade-Khalil Huffman
Infamous Landscapes	Prageeta Sharma
Bad Bad	Chelsey Minnis
Snip Snip!	Tina Brown Celona
Yes, Master	Michael Earl Craig
Swallows	Martin Corless-Smith
Folding Ruler Star	Aaron Kunin
The Commandrine & Other Poems	Joyelle McSweeney
Macular Hole	Catherine Wagner
Nota	Martin Corless-Smith
Father of Noise	Anthony McCann
Can You Relax in My House	Michael Earl Craig
Miss America	Catherine Wagner

FICTION

Prayer and Parable: Stories	Paul Maliszewski
Flet: A Novel	Joyelle McSweeney
The Mandarin	Aaron Kunin